Praise for the Books of Tony Mendoza

People Magazine, June 29, 1987
(Stories)

"There are word books and there are photo books, but rarely do the tw̲ mismatch. A notable exception is Mendoza's mating of paragraphs and ⌴⌴⌴⌴⌴ of 45 humorous and surprisingly poignant stepping-stones through his life ⌴⌴⌴⌴ shows in his self-deflating humor, as well as his book's (Stories) friendly size and price. Don't be deceived. This funny little book is as sophisticated and original as anything you'll find in the bookstore."

The New York Times Book Review, November 22, 1987
(Stories)

"Like all good autobiographers, Mr. Mendoza, a photographer of some renown, has constructed a persona. He's the outsider, a guy who uses his "aw shucks" naiveté and alienation to con people into laughing. He does it by writing short, self-deprecating, seductive sentences, the verbal equivalent of his photographs."

Los Angeles Times, Sunday March 12, 2000
(Cuba: Going Back)

"In his brilliant photographs, Mendoza doesn't betray any interest in the exile fantasies of return. He teases us, plays with our love of nostalgia, by bathing his black and white prints in sepia, making them look older, ...but, through his lens, Mendoza shows us the present disintegrating: An elderly man earns a few pesos filling cigarette lighters; the police checks a taxi driver's papers; a small boy plays baseball in the rubble; a sickly dog searches for scraps of food. What the gifted Mendoza delivers is the topography of a wasteland."

People Magazine, January 25, 1993
(Ernie: A Photographer's Memoir)

"One cat picture is worth a thousand meows--at least, if the photographer is Tony Mendoza. Mendoza practically invented a genre in 1985 with his enduring Ernie: A Photographer's Memoir. Crawling around a New York City loft for two years in pursuit of a rambunctious black and white cat, Mendoza produced a remarkable study of catness... With a clever narrative written from Ernie's viewpoint, the book never got cloying, or is that clawing? Ernie proved so popular that Mendoza followed up in 1989 with Ernie's Postcard Book. But the greatest tribute to the Ernie books is paid by their imitators."

Gustavo Perez Firmat, author, Life on the Hyphen
(A Cuban Summer, 2013)

Forget Ricky Ricardo, Forget Godfather II, Forget Hemingway. If you want to know what it was like to live in Havana during the 1950's, Tony Mendoza's absorbing novel is your best guide. Lively, sexy and beautifully written, A Cuban Summer is not only a sensitive (and ofter hilarious) coming of age tale but a splendid portrait of a culture and a way of life that would soon disappear, perhaps forever. Once I began the novel, I couldn't put it down."

ISBN: 978-0-692-93130-1

All photographs by Tony Mendoza except for the family album pictures on pages 6,7,8,9,13,14,89.

Book design by Tony Mendoza
Printed and Distributed by Thomson-Shore Inc.

Pictures with Stories

Tony Mendoza
2017

For JoAnn
Tony Mendoza
2019

My mother kept a detailed baby book for each of her five children. She wrote a brief description of anything interesting that happened in my life every month until I was eight. Sewn to my book is the green Parcheesi chip I swallowed when I was five months old.

Pictures with Stories

A Memoir by Tony Mendoza

My grandmother Otrín lived very happily with my grandfather for 51 years. They met at a party. She was sixteen. Her family had moved from Santiago and she was being introduced to Havana society. My grandfather asked her for a dance, and Otrín recalled, they barely talked, but she liked him. The next day my grandfather sent her a carriage filled with orchids; Otrín knew then that they would marry.

Mama, my maternal grandmother, was 86, widowed, and enjoying good health. Kiddingly, I said: "Mama, you look so young, why don't you get married again?" "Ay, hijo," she replied, "I've lived such a long and happy life. Your grandfather Papo was such a fine man, and I miss him so much. I'm ready now to go and join him." I said: "Mama, I know you are going to heaven, but are you sure Papo made it?" She laughed and said: "For 45 years he was a perfect husband. He's in heaven just for that."

My father, behind the stroke (who happened to be his brother Victor) in the undefeated 1933 Choate School varsity shell. That same year my mother decided that she was going to marry him. They went out on many dates, but four years later, when my father was about to graduate from Yale, and my mother figured the timing was right for him to propose, he was not proposing. My mother decided to take the initiative. She spread the news in Havana that my father had proposed. When my father returned to Havana, wherever he went, people congratulated him. At first, he would just say, thank you, thinking that they were referring to his Yale graduation. But then someone said; she's a beautiful woman. At first, he denied the news of the engagement but he claimed that no one believed him. Finally, he decided that it took a lot less effort to go along with the engagement story than to deny it. To this day, my mother remembers my father as the love of her life.

My father's best friends growing up were his three brothers. They went together to a camp in New Hampshire, then to Choate and Yale. At Yale they joined St. Elmo's, the wildest fraternity, partied nightly, and during the day they played varsity sports and maybe, attended classes. After college, they continued the good times, making the rounds of Havana parties as available and highly desirable bachelors. They acquired a nickname, the Eaton Boys. They were rich, good-looking, smart, educated, and they knew how to enjoy life. But then, the Eaton Boys party came to an end—they got married. Still, they could not bear staying apart, so they all went to work for their father at the sugar mill he built and managed in Camaguey province, lived together in the large family house, and started their families. Every night after dinner my father and uncles would disappear into the game room to drink scotch and play bridge. From my bedroom one floor above I could hear them yelling, screaming, laughing, and arguing wildly after every hand. I apparently didn't inherit their boisterousness. I'm the serious looking blond boy sitting on the floor.

During the Forties, my mother took me to photographer's studios or photographers came to our house every time she felt she needed more pictures for her baby books. The best one in Havana, according to my mother, was a photographer who called himself Rembrandt. This is one of his pictures, a black and white picture of my sister Margarita and I, which Rembrandt hand colored. I agree with my mother that he was very good, although he got carried away painting our eyes too blue. When I look at the picture, I can't help thinking of the movie: Children of the Corn! I'm also thinking: I can honestly say that I own a Rembrandt.

My fourth grade class picture at Belen, Havana's largest Jesuit school and Fidel Castro's alma mater. Brother Ignacio, the sacred history teacher, did not allow boys to go to the bathroom during class. One day I needed to pee badly. I raised my hand and explained my problem. Brother Ignacio listened and said: no. Instead, he asked me to stand in front of the class and read from the sacred history textbook. Halfway through the reading I couldn't hold it any more. I brought the book very close to my face and stopped reading. The pee stained my pants, then trickled down my leg, and went down the wooden platform's three steps. The class was dead silent at first. Then they started laughing, somewhat nervously, and their laughter grew louder and louder, as if I was the funniest thing they had ever seen. I stood there frozen, now the book firmly pressed against my face.

I was ten years old, spending my first summer away from home at Camp Pasquaney in New Hampshire. Every Monday the campers would climb a different mountain in the White Mountains range. When I got to the top I would take out my Brownie and take four pictures; north, south, east, and west. Once a week I mailed the drugstore prints to my parents in Cuba, who were eager to know how I was doing. All I would write in my extremely short letters: Hello. I'm having a great time. This is the mountain I climbed this week. Love. Tony.

When we were thirteen, in 1954, Machete and I were sent to Choate, a Connecticut all-boys prep school. We quickly became best friends and also managed to have more than our share of reckless teenage adventures. High up on the list; on Christmas vacation we decided that we were old enough, at thirteen, to go to the Mambo Club, one of Havana's more elegant brothels. And even worse, a few years later we met two American girls our age vacationing in Havana. After some spirited dates with necking sessions, we all decided we were in love. Unfortunately, their vacation ended and the girls returned to their homes in Miami. Machete convinced me that we needed to continue the festivities. The next day, after leaving notes on our beds, we left for Miami at 4 am from the Havana Yacht Club, in Machete's 14-foot aluminum outboard. We took sandwiches, water, a compass, a map, a 22-rifle, a few fishing lines and enough gasoline. What we didn't plan for was for our outboard motor to die after an hour, with the Cuban coastline barely visible. We were bobbing like a cork in huge swells, thinking we had done something really stupid. A few hours later, the Cuban coast guard found us and picked us up.

When I started paying attention to girls in Varadero Beach, Magda, Tota, and Ma-
nana used to make me nervous. Every time I saw them, they were always laughing. I was afraid to talk to them and run the risk of not being considered funny.

In 1957 my sister Margarita's debut party was held in an elegant stage set in the courtyard of the Havana Yacht Club. This picture was taken during the father/daughter dance, and I can see that my father is stepping on Margarita's dress on the top left of the frame. I remember talking that year with friends my age about Fidel Castro, who was then leading a guerrilla war in the mountains of Oriente province. Cuban politicians were all crooks, we agreed, and if Fidel somehow managed to topple Batista, he would turn out into another crook. He turned into something else. Three years after Margarita's debut party, 99% of the membership of the Havana Yacht Club, including my family, found themselves living in Miami, in drastically reduced circumstances.

I found this slightly out of focus snapshot taken at my Yale graduation in 1963. To my right, wearing a huge necklace, Helenita M., my girlfriend during my senior year at Yale. I was head over heels in love with Helenita. After graduation, I thought I had my future all figured out. I had an engineering degree, and a job lined up designing railroad bridges for the New York Central railroad. (I made sure in the ensuing years to never take a train that crossed the bridge I had designed.) My plan was to work for one year as an engineer, save money (I rented a slum apartment in the Lower East Side for $75 a month,) apply to graduate architectural school, and prepare for it by taking night art courses at the Cooper Union. Meanwhile, Helenita went to Paris to do a year abroad. I was assuming that when Helenita returned from Paris we would take it up where we had left off. The romantic part of my plan didn't work out. Helenita sent me as kind a letter as possible but it said; I've met someone new. I'm sorry. Our thing is over. I was a heartbroken wreck for nine months. Then I moved to Cambridge, started architecture school at Harvard, met all sort of interesting grad students. My life moved on.

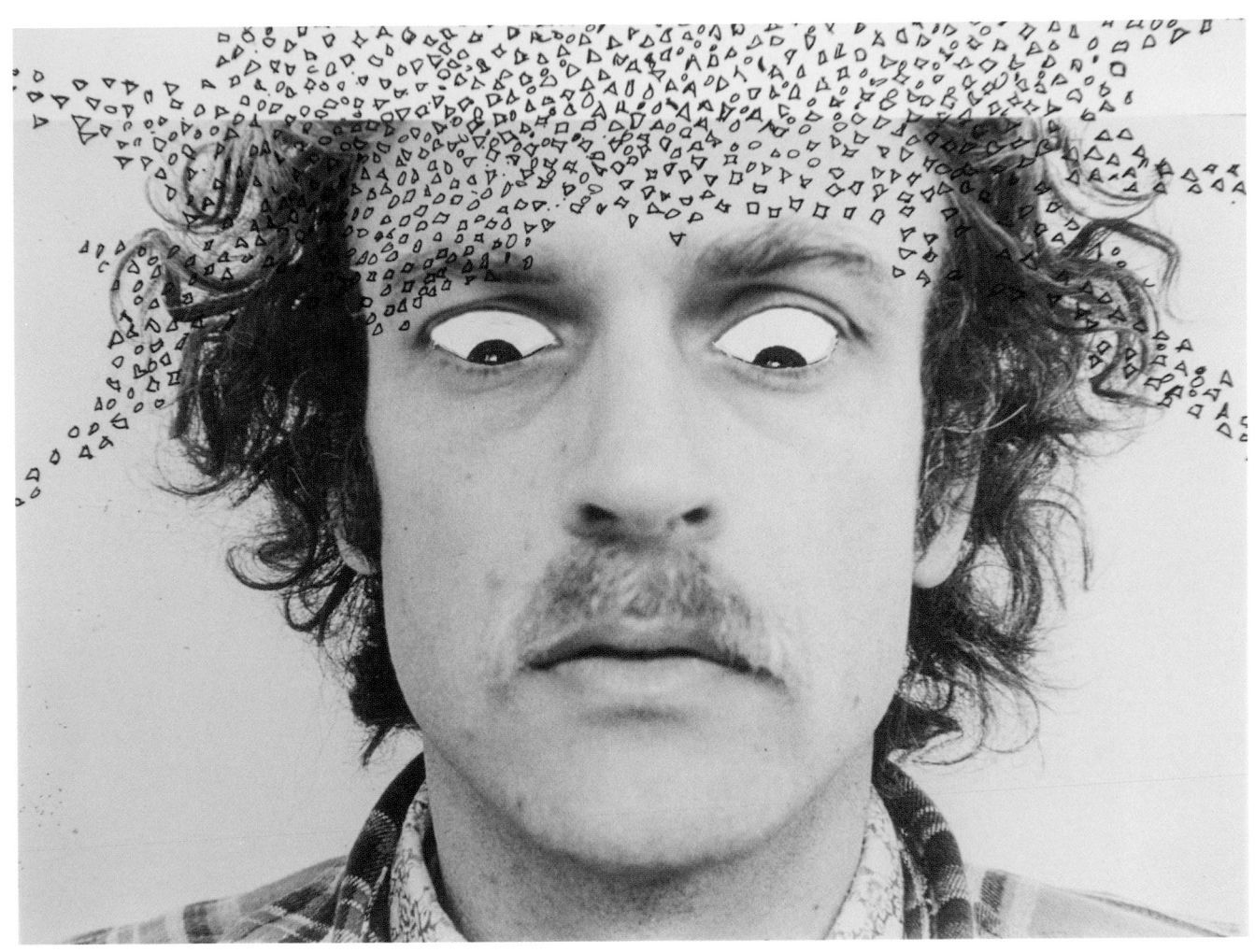

In 1967 I dropped out of graduate school for six months so I could move to San Francisco and experience what was going on over there. I especially wanted to be there for what was being promoted as "The Summer of Love." Another classmate had a Porche convertible and together we drove cross-country, our hair flying in the wind, while the song constantly on the radio advised; "If you are going to San Francisco, be sure to wear some flowers in your hair…" We didn't want to totally drop out, so we got architectural jobs during the week, and found an apartment near the Haight-Ashbury. On weekends, we headed for Golden Gate Park and did what everyone else was doing; meeting people, lying around on blankets, smoking joints, talking, and listening to music. At some point that summer I made friends with a group of hippies who liked to camp out on the banks of Mad River and drop acid. All I know for certain about The Summer of Love is that now I have fewer brain cells.

In 1970, for one year, I traveled in Europe with no set itinerary. Usually, I would meet an interesting group of like-minded travelers and wherever they were going next, I would tag along. Every day was a welcomed surprise. At some point, I ran out of money and got a job working for an architect in Paris. Then, when the summer started I hit the road again and ended up in the Greek islands, where I taught myself to do watercolors. I also learned that taking Greek ferries and traveling fourth class, on the roof, was an almost guaranteed adventure. I could count on finding up there ex-hippies from all over the world, sitting in groups, passing joints around. It was easy to join a group, make friends, and find a traveling companion, preferably female, with whom I would explore the island until one or the other decided to take another ferry, meet someone new on the roof, and the process would repeat itself. I treasure my memories of that year, but now, I included one large regret—it was the last time I was totally focused on being adventuresome and free.

In 1973 I decided to give photography, a life-long hobby, a shot. I figured I would do "photojournalism" and to get started I needed to go somewhere dangerous, so I went to Colombia. I traveled all over, mostly to small towns, took pictures, and paid locals one dollar to string my hammock on their porch, and another dollar if they feed me breakfast or lunch. This picture was taken in Palenque, an isolated town deep in a swampy area, where an African dialect was still spoken. The small towns were perfectly safe, but the roads were full of bandits. I was robbed three times while traveling, at knifepoint, at gunpoint and at machine gun point. By the end of the trip I had lost all my photo equipment and most of my courage. After that trip, I was never interested in doing photojournalism again.

I started photographing in the early Seventies, at the height of the anti-war demonstrations. In one of my ventures into activist photography demonstrators attempted to block the entry to the Kennedy Building in Boston's Government Center. I found it amusing that a riot cop's helmet was numbered 1984, and he became my photographic project that day. He didn't seem to understand why I so persistently photographed him, but clearly, he didn't like it. When demonstrators refused to budge after repeated warnings, the cops were given the go-ahead, and they charged, clubs swinging. 1984 came rushing straight for me, and chased me the length of Government Center, but I outran him.

In 1972 I approached a young woman in Harvard Square who was promoting her spiritual leader, the fifteen-year-old Perfect Master, the Guru Maharajah Ji. I told her I was willing to listen only if I could take a picture of her hands. She agreed, I took the picture, then she told me how perfect the Perfect Master was, and how he had changed her life. As she spoke, she brought her face very close to mine, maybe within two or three inches, making me feel very uncomfortable, even paranoid. I was thinking that this was some Eastern brainwashing technique. One year later, I read with interest how the Perfect Master had accumulated a world-class collection of toys.

In 1970 I moved into an urban commune in the Boston area and lived there throughout the decade of the Seventies. There must have been over one hundred communes in the Boston area that sprang up at that time, but our group was different in that almost everyone was a professional; lawyers, anthropologists, architects, computer professionals, psychologists, and the press loved it. They picked us up as an upbeat "new age" story and we were written up by magazines and even appeared in a segment of CBS 60 Minutes. Most of the original members had met in an encounter group/sensitivity awareness workshop and after buying a 12-bedroom house and moving in, we continued to hold weekly encounter sessions, where all house or personal tensions would be aired and discussed. Overcoming sexual hang-ups was a big deal at that time. A new bathtub had two shower heads, one at each end, designed to encourage bathing in pairs. We built a large sauna in the basement and used it nightly before festive dinners hosted by rotating cooks; we joked that whenever we wanted to see someone naked, all we had to do was invite him (or her) for dinner.

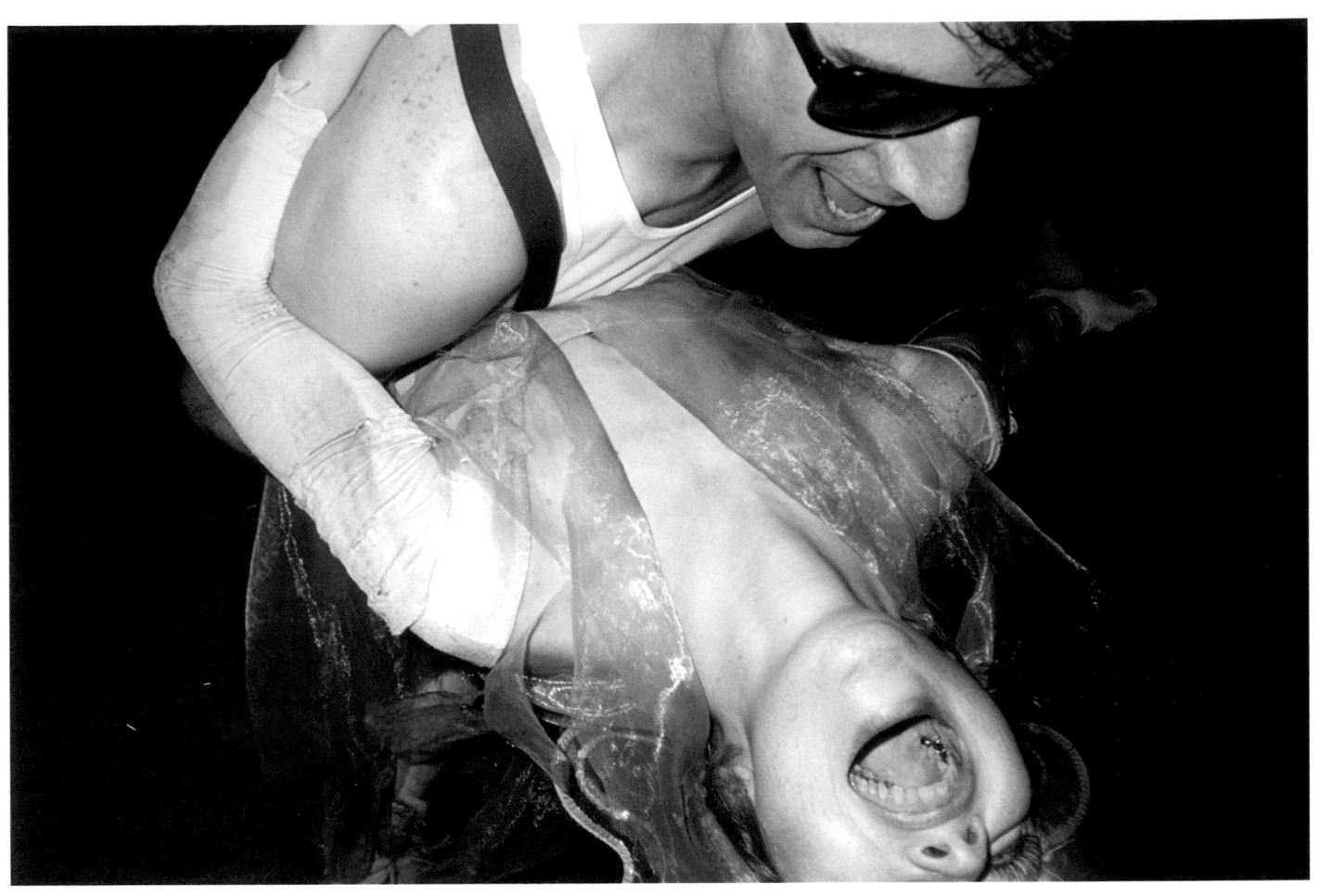

Our house became known for great dancing parties. A local speaker company would set up with their latest high-end equipment and a music committee of house members would spend a week coming up with the ultimate dance tape. The year we decided not to hold our traditional New Year's dance party, 75 people still showed up.

In 1973 I quit my job as an architect and became an artist. I hated the routine of having to go to work every day and particularly, having to get up at seven in the morning. I always felt tired and would yawn throughout the day. I became convinced that waking up to an alarm clock was unnatural and would shorten my life. On my last day of work I walked to the tip of Lewis Wharf and threw my watch and alarm clock into Boston Harbor.

available, may I suggest that you contact a reputable lending
institution and secure the amount to pay this indebtedness.

By prompt attention to this matter, you can avoid the inconven-
ience and expense associated with the forthcoming lawsuit.

Very truly yours,

Francis C. Newton

Francis C. Newton
Attorney for Plai

Dear Mr. Mendoza,

Thank you for your monthly payments of $5.00
however, your loan account is seriously in a.
no longer accept payments less than your co
is $29.86.

Please begin monthly payments of $29.86
be appreciated if you would contact me to ma

Dear Mr. Mendoza:

Many letters have been sent to you regar
student loan account, we have had no rep

account will be turned over to a co
unless we hear from you within tw

RE: Antonio Mendoza
VS. Harvard University Student L
DEFENDANT
BALANCE DUE: $ 495.38

2 Summit Ave.
omerville, Mass.

Re: Harvard Coop. So
Amount due: $238,

Please be advised that I represent the above-name
creditor in a claim against you in the amount indicated.

This balance, being long overdue, I mu
either payment in full be made immediately, or that y
office for a suitable arrangement of payment. Delay
of these will leave me no alternative but to institut
ings for the collection of this indebtedness.

Please make your check payable to me a
directly to this office.

As a result of your continued failure to liquidate
above referenced account, we have, this day, advise
client legal proceedings against you are their only
recourse.

Upon their agreement, we will forward your account
attorney in your area to take appropriate legal act

Following up on our telephone conversation of this af
noon I have enclosed a hardship deferment for you. P
complete it and send it to us as soon as possible.

As I mentioned on the telephone it must be accompanie
a certified copy of your income tax return, which may
received from the I.R.S., however, as this is time-co
send your hardship form, along with a copy of your ta

I attended five years of private school, four years of college, and three years of
graduate school before I became an architect. In 1973, five years after graduation, I
quit architecture and became an artist-photographer. For the next ten years, I never
earned more than $8,000 a year. In 1977 some college loans came due. In addition,
I defaulted on my charge cards and my "Evergreen" bank account. After a while,
creditors grew impatient and handed over my accounts to collection agencies. After
receiving many threatening letters, I politely informed everyone that I was now an artist and continually broke and should be considered a total loss. I kept receiving their
threatening letters. Finally, I sent each a collage of their letters with a contact strip of
myself eating a banana. I never heard from my creditors again.

Anne and I were a couple in the commune. We didn't believe in being possessive or jealous and enjoyed a satisfying relationship for two years. When we separated, we decided we were mature enough to stay in the house and deal with the difficult feelings surrounding new mates. Anne became involved with Mark, another man in the house. I became possessive and jealous.

My father, a businessman, thoroughly disapproved of my artistic life-style, my financial irresponsibility, my failure to get married and raise a family, and he didn't understand art. Then, during the early Seventies, Richard Nixon became his favorite political person and I became equally convinced that Nixon was emotionally disturbed. On my visits to my parents, my father and I would start out talking about safe subjects, but as the evening and scotches progressed, we would grow bolder and start discussing Watergate. Within minutes the discussion would deteriorate into a yelling match wherein the winner would be judged solely on volume.

When I first moved into the commune, I built a darkroom in the basement. For the next five years, I worked full time at getting better at the craft of darkroom photography, took classes and workshops with well-known photographers, and did innumerable self-assigned art photography projects. Nevertheless, I wasn't having much success finding a gallery that would show my work, or a publisher that would publish it. After repeated rejections I was close to giving up on photography and going back to architecture when I came up with a project that gave me some hope. I printed a group of pictures I had done in Florida and hand toned one part of the black and white prints with a brown toner. I liked the results and I was not alone. The Fogg Museum bought a few pictures, a gallery gave me a small show, and I never again considered going back to architecture.

During the last year I was in the commune, I photographed my girlfriend's dog, a large black dog named Leela. I would take her out for walks at the end of the day and noticed that when I photographed her with flash, the backgrounds would go to black and the dog would be highlighted. I really liked the results and decided to try to put together a Leela portfolio. Leela knew all the neighborhood dogs and she played with them. Her favorite game was the game of stick. The rules called for holding on to the stick while never looking directly at your opponent.

Casey and Leela, were best friends. The second before I took this picture, they were playing with a stick, each dog clamping on it hoping to win the game by ending up with it. For some reason, I remembered the iconic picture of a scowling Winston Churchill taken in 1941 by Yousuf Karsh, one of the most widely reproduced photographs of all time. Churchill, who was a busy man, gave Karsh two minutes to take the picture. He came in and stood in front of the view camera, smoking his ever-present cigar. Karsh didn't like his contented expression. He went up to Churchill, yanked the cigar out of his mouth, and clicked the shutter. I did the same. I yanked the stick out of their mouths and clicked. This picture has been used to illustrate various magazine articles, including an article on the strange behavior of animals before an earthquake.

I moved to New York City in 1980. At first, I supported myself by selling Leela pictures to magazines, collectors and museums. My best seller was the world's only picture of a very large dog about to attack an ant.

I moved to Manhattan thinking that I needed to be there to make it in the art world. I was very lucky to find what was probably the last affordable loft in Tribeca, and it had a darkroom. The loft was on the last floor, and the windows gave to the roof, where I liked to go out at night to photograph Ernie, our loft cat. On the first floor of our building was the Odeon Restaurant, which probably defined the New York night scene during the 80s, the hang out of John Belushi, who seemed to be there every night, as well as Warhol, Basquiat, Mapplethorpe, and Jay McInerney, who captured that coke infused world in his novel *Bright Lights, Big City.* During the four years I lived in the loft I was failing miserably to make it in the art world, constantly broke, and too poor to eat or drink in the Odeon, but every night while I waited for the outside elevator to come down, I would look in through the large plate glass windows and watch all the celebrities having a great time, all high on something, or their good fortune. The elevator would arrive; I would go upstairs and hang out with the cat.

After I had lived in the loft for one year, I had accumulated a growing list of debts to credit cards. I realized I had to do some commercial photography. Initially, my book, what I showed art directors to get work, had a good amount of portraits, mostly family portraits, and I got some jobs doing portraits for magazines and a few small newspapers. Then my book started filling up with a disproportionate amount of cat pictures, since all the photography I was doing in the loft were pictures of Ernie, and I thought they were good, so I put them in. To my dismay, art directors progressively pegged me as a cat photographer, and the number of jobs I was called to do dropped precipitously. For this cover, I tried to sell them an Ernie cover, but the art director insisted I photograph her own cat. Ernie was not pleased.

I lived in Tribeca for four years and I always had a problem coming up with the rent. My portion wasn't much for a New York loft, around $700, but I was always short when the rent payment came around. On the last Saturday of every month I would set up at the corner of Broome Street and West Broadway and would sell 16x20 inch Ernie pictures for $50 until I met the rent shortfall. As the day progressed, if the pictures weren't moving enough at $50, I would lift the paper sign on the brick wall and under it was a $40 sign. I would always sell some at $40, but if it was getting late and I was still short on the rent, I would lift the paper sign again to expose the $30 sign. The cat pictures always moved fast at $30. One day a curator from the Museum of Modern Art came by and said: "We have this picture of Ernie chasing the dragonfly in our collection. What you are doing is very bad for your career." I agreed, somewhat embarrassed, but I had rent to pay. In 2016, some 36 years after they collected it, I got an email from MoMA saying that the Ernie and the dragonfly picture (as well as the dog and the ant picture) will be among the 53 collection works included in the 2018 Museum of Modern Art Appointment Calendar. Whoever bought it for $30 will be surprised.

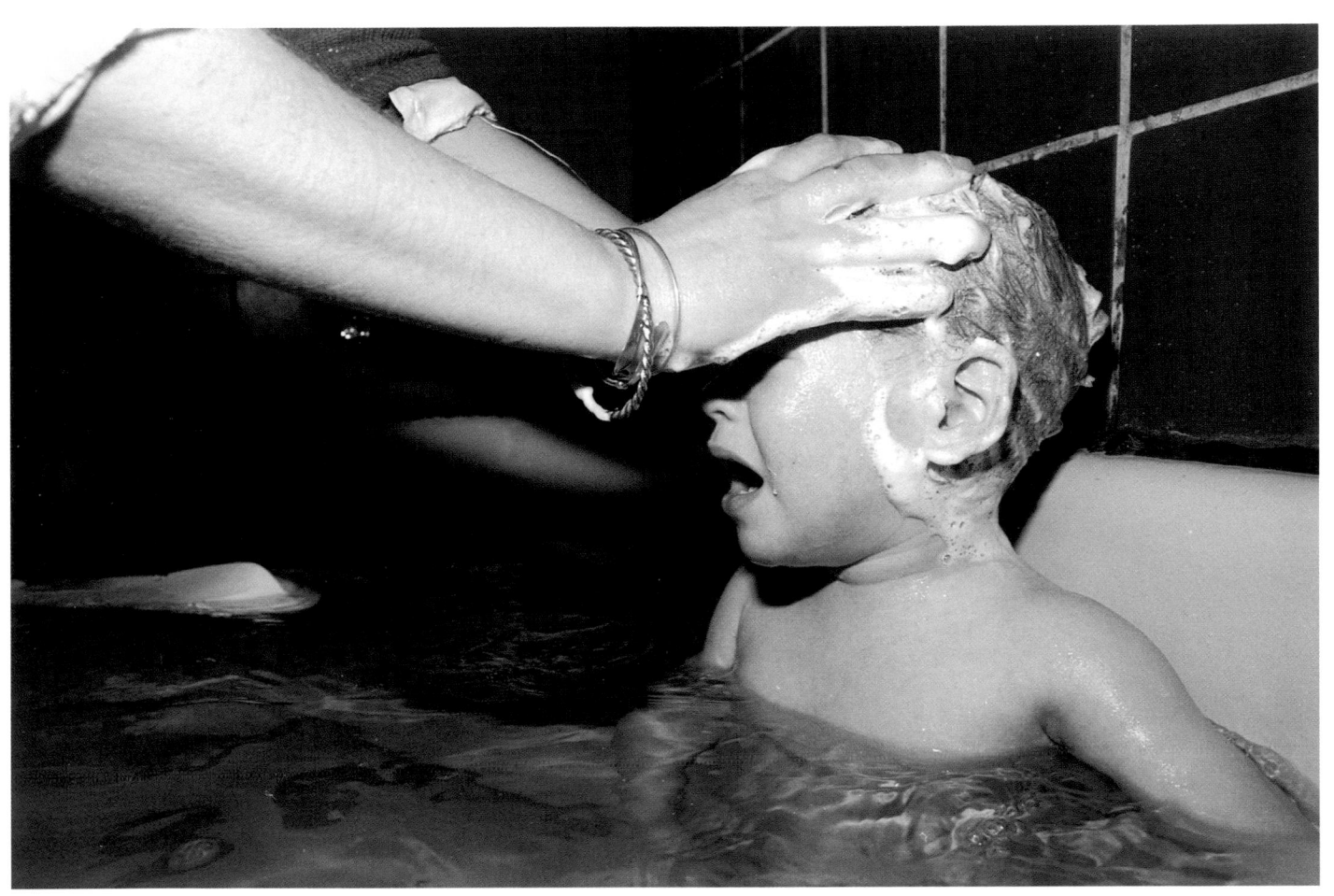

WORKING MOTHER

November 3, 1982

Dear Mr. Mendoza:

Thank you for bringing in your portfolio for me to see. Your interest in our magazine is appreciated. However, in all honesty, I can't foresee an opportunity to use the kind of photography that you do. Rarely do we work with real people, and the people that we do use are not characterized in the way that they are in your book. Good luck placing your photography elsewhere.

Cordially,

In New York the only photography jobs I cheerfully accepted were weddings. I was fascinated by people in love, and liked to watch them, hoping to gain some insights into the state of mind that allows a man or woman to look at their partner and say, yes, I want to be with this person for the rest of my life.

I had an Ernie show at the Witkin gallery in Soho in 1988. After the show closed, a man called the gallery and told them that he wanted me to photograph his cat. The gallery suggested he call me because I lived in Ohio. He called and asked me if I could fly to New York the next weekend, photograph his cat, and his two dogs. What would I charge? I wasn't prepared for the question, so I started by telling him that he would first have to pay for my plane ticket to New York. He quickly said, "no problem," which made me think that he was probably well off, so I thought I should go for a price on the high side. So I blurted out $1800 for three 16x20 prints. I immediately regretted it, thinking I had been too greedy. No problem, he said again. I told him I would be crawling around on the floor of his apartment for a full day. Would he mind that? No, he said. He gave me his address. The next weekend I flew to New York. When I asked the doorman for his apartment number, on a building next to Central Park, he said, it's the penthouse. The penthouse had a huge terrace with a Japanese Garden. The walls featured a large number of famous artists as well as vintage 19th-century photographs that I recognized from history books. While I was crawling around on the floor, taking pictures of the dogs and the cat, two dealers came in trying to sell the collector some 19th century photographs. The prices being mentioned were, in my opinion, astronomical. The dealers kept looking at me on the floor, wondering what the hell was going on. I printed this picture of his cat. He liked it. Later, I figured I could have charged more.

A frame filled with my relatives, during the party the night before Sergio Mendoza and Enid Duany's wedding. Most members of my family are talkers, and almost everyone is a drinker. Family parties tend to be loud.

I introduced Hervin to his first wife, Cindy, when Hervin and I were roommates in Paris in 1970. They were married within a year, but three years later they divorced. In 1975 I introduced Hervin to my cousin Ana Maria during the party she gave for Sergio Mendoza and Enid Duany. The party was progressing admirably. Hervin, drink in hand, was surveying the crowd when someone passing in front of him forced him slightly backwards into a large chrome and glass bookcase overloaded with Steuben glass animals, framed photographs, books, and it all came crashing down. Broken glass was everywhere and the party ended shortly afterwards. In Ana Maria's eyes, Hervin was the culprit and she was furious at him for weeks. Nevertheless, Hervin did a great job of apologizing. They were married three years later.

My parents came to Boston in 1968 for my graduation from architectural school. After the ceremony, my father, who loved lobster, wanted to celebrate in one of Boston's seafood restaurants. We ordered a table, but the headwaiter informed us that we couldn't be served because I wasn't wearing a tie. Earlier that year I had decided that ties were a symbol of the establishment. My father, who was outspoken, started screaming, furious at the restaurant, and especially, at me. Nevertheless, I didn't wear a tie again till 1983. While I was visiting Ana Maria and Hervin in Florida, we were invited to a wedding. I borrowed a white suit, shirt, and tie from Hervin. Looking at myself in the mirror, I felt unusually opulent and handsome. During the party that night, I noticed women looking at me often. Afterward, I started wearing suits and ties.

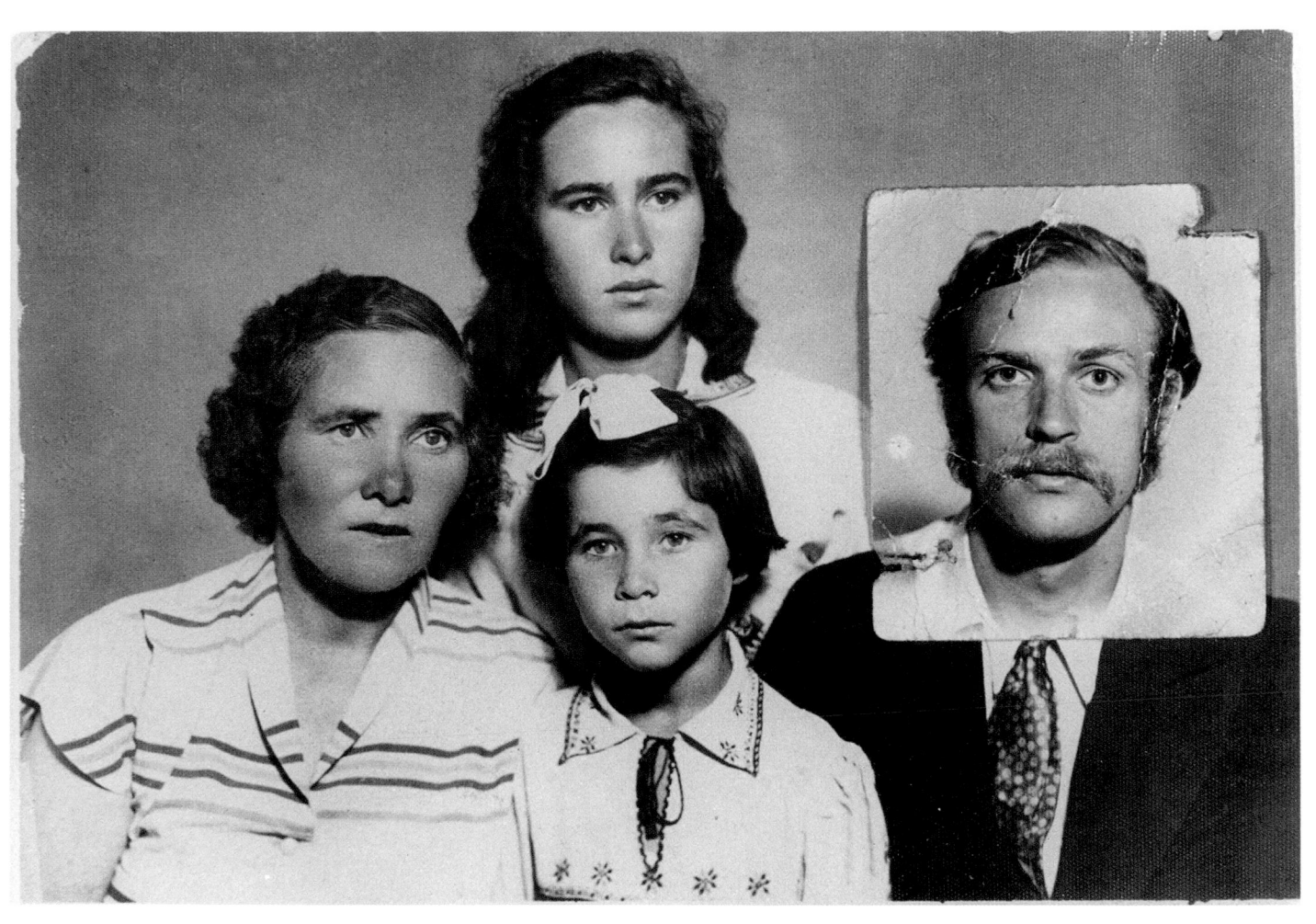

I had always liked the idea of having a family, but never felt emotionally or financially ready. When I turned 42, I started thinking that I was emotionally and financially unable to remain single.

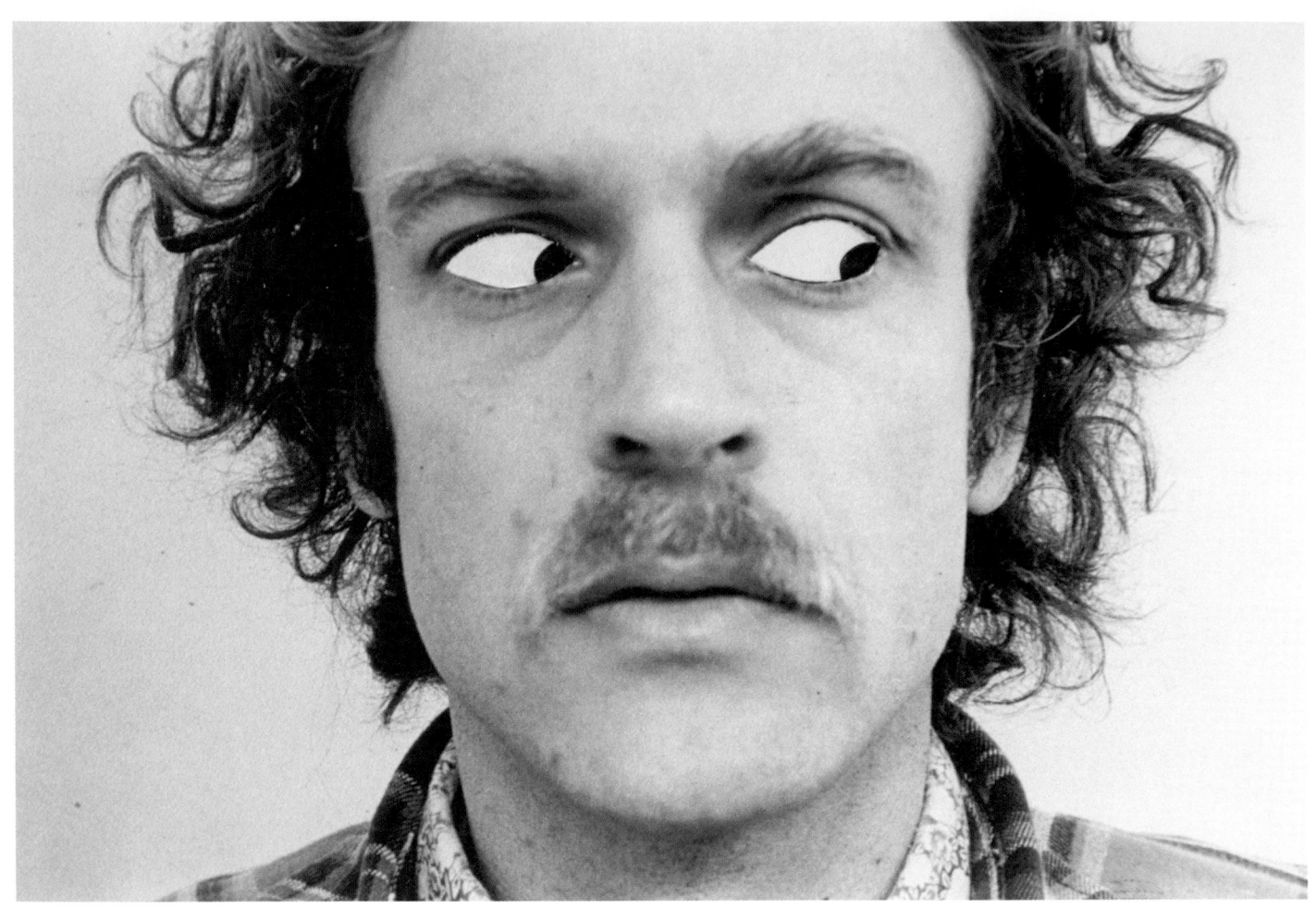

The day I turned 43, I had a feeling that at some point in my life I had taken the wrong turn. I found myself at a place I didn't particularly want to be: an unknown artist, never married, unable to sustain relationships, without health insurance, and I had to move to my sister's house in Brooklyn when they more than doubled the rent on the Tribeca loft. I wondered, what can go wrong next? That night I got so depressed that I went out and bought a few bottles of wine and got falling-down drunk. My mood improved considerably a few weeks later when I got a call from the secretary at MoMA's photography department. She said that John Szarkowski, the photography curator, liked the portfolio of pictures with stories I had dropped off so much that he wanted to buy the 65 phtographs in the box. John wanted to meet me and discuss the project and the price. Sure, I said, I can meet with him. I hung up. Then I yelled so loudly and for so long that the neighbors must have thought I won the lottery. Then another very good thing happened.

I met Carmen at a party in Boston in 1979. The hostess introduced us by saying, you two have something in common, and then walked away. It turned out we had many things in common. Carmen was a liberal/progressive Cuban exile, had an interest in art after studying art history at BU, and was now curious about getting in touch with her Cuban roots. We enjoyed an instant relationship, but it came to an end when I moved to NYC in 1980 to pursue an art career, and Carmen moved to California. Over the next four years we regularly kept in touch, mostly through postcards and letters, even though she married a new age guru, moved to Hawaii with him, and had a son. In 1984 she separated from the guru, and returned to her mother's house in New York. She called me, and at dinner that night we knew that we were going to end up together. When I won a Guggenheim Fellowship in 1985, we decided to use some of the money to leave New York and move to Miami. It was a good move. We especially enjoyed living near a warm ocean, the Miami winters, the terrific Cuban restaurants in Little Havana, and our many Cuban relatives, who never failed to ask us: "When are you two getting married?" We also liked the house we rented at the edge of Coral Gables. Every late afternoon we drank mojitos by our back garden, and like clockwork, around seven, a flock of boisterous wild parrots would land on one of our trees.

Carmen, the day before we were married in 1986 in Key Biscayne, Florida. I was lucky that this smart, attractive and kind woman would put up with me after my 45-year-long extended adolescence and bachelorhood.

Carmen didn't quite know what she was getting into marrying an always-on-the-job photographer. I figured that my wedding was an excellent opportunity for a photo project so I set up a studio just outside the function room in the Key Biscayne hotel where we were married. After the ceremony, I photographed the long-married couples that came to our wedding and took notes for the text, after asking them for tips on how to succeed at marriage. We went to Cozumel for our honeymoon and I made her submerge with me for more than a few takes so I could get a good underwater portrait—which later became the postcard we sent as a thank-you-note for our wedding presents.

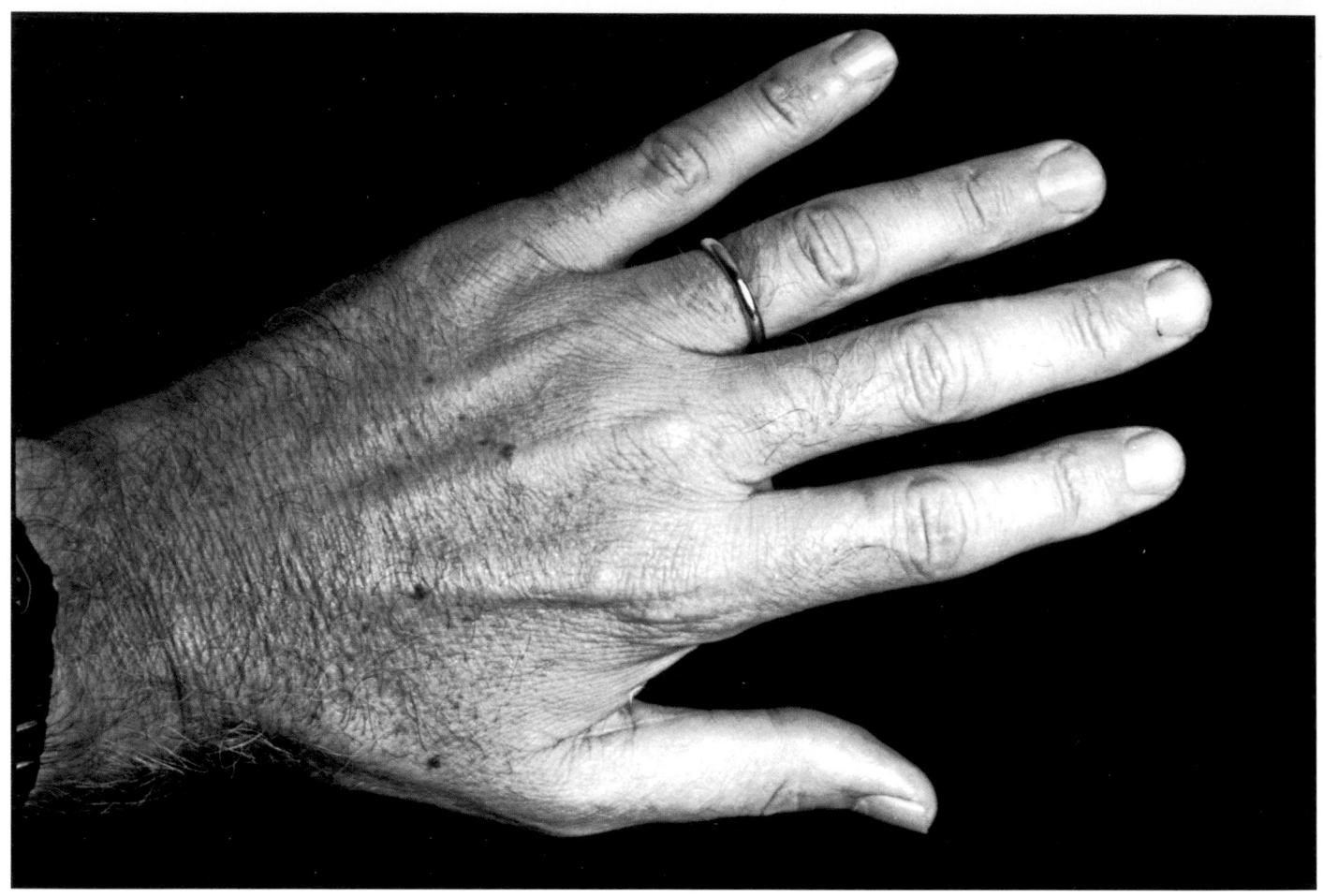

Initially, I resisted the idea of wearing a wedding band, mostly because I had never worn a ring and I didn't understand jewelry, but when Carmen insisted, I agreed. After a while, I started to enjoy wearing the band: it reminded me of my new status as married and "grown up," a status I liked. I especially enjoyed tapping the ring on the roof of the car as I drove, to the rhythms of Cuban music. Two months after we were married, Carmen and I went swimming in Key Biscayne, and driving home afterward I started tapping the roof and realized that the ring was missing. The following day, early in the morning when the water was calm, we went back to the beach. Finding the ring in water up to our chests seemed hopeless, and we gave up. One month later, at the same beach, we noticed a man in the water with a metal detector. Carmen suggested we give him our phone number in case he found the ring, which had Carmen's name inscribed on it. That night he called. He said he had found it 200 yards from where I told him I'd been swimming, and one foot under the surface of the sand.

When I lived in Miami, this is what I did for work. I took pictures of my family, my cat, myself. I printed the pictures and submitted them for grants. With the grant money I rented a place by the ocean. I sat at the water's edge and photographed my toes. I printed the picture and wrote under it a story about what I did for work.

One year after Carmen and I were married, I realized that my days as a free-lance photographer were over. Alex had a terrible case of stomach flu. He couldn't stop vomiting, and had to spend two days in a Miami hospital. The hospital bill came to $3000 dollars. After I paid, I knew that I had to get a regular job, with health insurance. It took a while, but finally Ohio State offered me a job teaching photography. "Can you teach sensitometry," they asked. "Sure," I replied. After the phone call I rushed to the library to find out what sensitometry was.

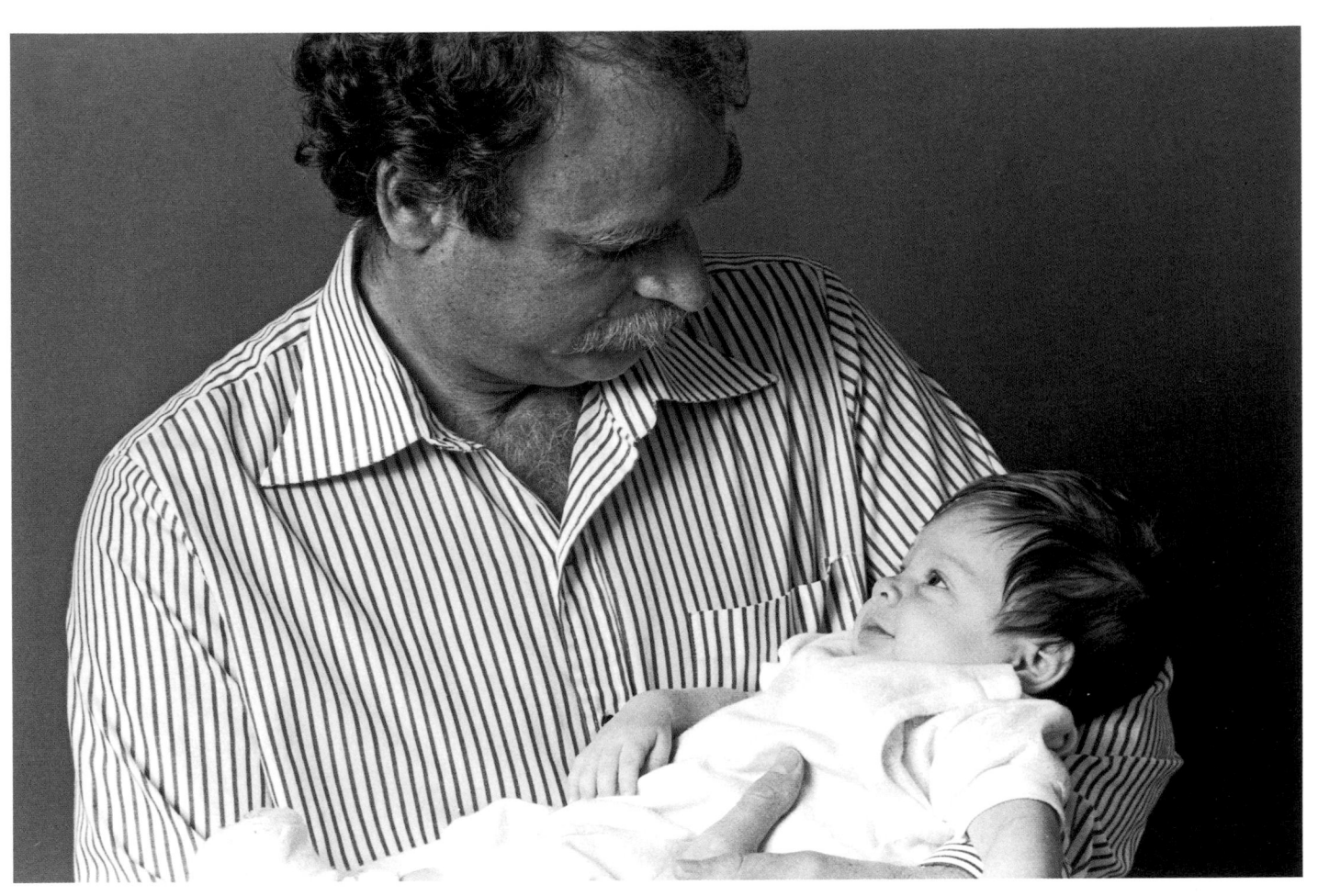

Lydia, my first (and only) child was born when I was 47. I realized then that I had waited too long. When I held her in my arms, she was out of focus.

Halloween, 1992. Lydia, who had just turned three, wanted to be a bride.

Halloween, 1992. The neighbors.

Halloween, 1998. Lydia wanted to be Cleopatra, Queen of the Nile.

Halloween 2000. Audrey Hepburn.

April 20,1993. The best expression I could come up with the day after I was diagnosed with leukemia.

June 21, 2011. Eighteen years after I was diagnosed with leukemia, my white cell count is normal. The high white cell count that led to the diagnosis went down every year, without treatment. Now I only go in for a yearly blood test every June. I had been meaning to ask my doctor if maybe I was misdiagnosed, and finally I did ask him this June. He said: "No, you still have CLL, but you're doing great." My theory: I had a case of selenium poisoning. I selenium toned all my black and white prints when I did darkroom photography. I was supposed to use gloves while toning the prints, because selenium when used in photography is toxic, but I rarely did. After I turned to digital and stopped doing darkroom work, my high white cell count steadily declined.

I did a lot of worrying after I was diagnosed. For a number of years, it was difficult to have an optimistic thought about the future. Carmen, thinking she might end up as the sole wage earner in the family, went back to school, got a Master's in education, and became a teacher. My thoughts about the future are now back to normal, but I worry about other things. I have a theory that I have a worry quota that I always have to fill. Still, my worries at 70 are not so bad. I don't worry about dying. I'm finding it difficult to find something to seriously worry about, but here is my list. I still teach, and I worry about not being a good teacher, especially in a university art department where everything is about the new and the latest. I still try to make new work, but I worry about being a viable artist when I'm not much of a postmodernist. I also can't seem to get a New York gallery to show my work, or even to look at it. Carmen and I usually get along great, but I worry about the times when we don't. Our kids, Lydia and Alex are great kids, but I worry about their economic future. Lydia graduated from Vassar this June, a biology major, and she can't find a job. None of her classmates have been able to get jobs either. Alex graduated from Ohio State six years ago and has a dead-end job. But he has a great sense of humor and is educated and smart, so I am confident he will find his way. I always worry about money. I never seem to have enough. But that is normal.

At this very moment, I have a minor health problem. I'm a tennis fanatic. Early this summer I tore my Achilles tendon playing tennis. I was running hard for a ball, missed it, and then felt a very sharp pain in the back of my leg. My first thought was that my partner, who is famous in Columbus for his bad temper, threw his racquet at me in disgust when I missed the shot. I had surgery, and after a couple of weeks of lying around with my leg bandaged up, I went to the surgeon's office to get a cast put on. I was surprised to be presented, like in a paint store, with a little book of 12 color samples. I was torn between yellow and blue and finally a blue cast won out.

In 1996, I went to Cuba, my first trip back since leaving in 1960. I couldn't ignore the longing I felt to see again the places of my childhood and teenage years. One of my first destinations was my family's summer house in Varadero Beach. As I got closer to the house, I expected to see a ruin, since many of the houses I walked by were gutted. When I got there I was pleasantly surprised: our house was in perfect condition, just as the day I left it. It was a government guest house. The front door was open. I walked in and found a young woman on the porch that overlooks the ocean, playing a saxophone with her eyes closed. I liked the scene, and the melody of the song she was playing. She opened her eyes and found me there. We talked. Her band was staying in the house. She offered to give me a tour of the house, and afterward, I went down to the water. There was no one on the fine sand beach. I put all my clothes in a pile on the sand with the camera on top, and went in. I was in the water for a while, looking towards the house. The house next to ours, the del Valle house, had disappeared, and in its place there was a large pile of sand. I remembered those days when this beach was populated by relatives and friends and there was a constant din of motorboats and children's voices and I was so happy to be spending summers in our house by the sea.

During the two weeks I was in Cuba, I found a socialist system that was spectacularly dysfunctional. Most Cubans worked for the government, at a salary equivalent to 15 dollars a month, and no one seemed to do any work. This coffee shop attendant had nothing to do since he had nothing to sell. He told me that his shop was the unofficial neighborhood confessional. All day long people stopped by and told him their problems.

Photographs are inherently surreal objects, and photographs taken in Cuba tend to be doubly surreal. What does this picture explain? Very little, or a lot. Some general decided that more tourists would go to Cuba if they created a unique dinosaur park in the mountains of Oriente province. So, I'm assuming, without doing much further market research on this idea, they put to work an army of craftsmen to construct life-size dinosaurs, sprinkled them all over this desolate landscape, and waited for the tourists to come. The day I went, I was the only tourist there, and then a man bicycled by.

I took this picture in a Cuban park. At first I thought he was a male nanny taking care of the child of a high party official, since the park was next to an exclusive residential area and most Cuban high party officials are white. I was mistaken. This is a grandfather and his grandchild. Was the grandfather a descendent of blacks and his grandchild turned out lily-white? Not really. The grandfather is as lily-white as the child, but he has worked in the fields, and his skin is permanently tanned. Does the child hand gesture remind one of Renaissance paintings of baby Jesus? Maybe, but the grandchild is a girl.

In 2003 I decided that 30 years of doing only black and white darkroom photography was long enough. I needed to work digitally and in color. I bought a Nikon D70 and an Epson wide printer. On my first outing with the new camera I wanted to photograph something colorful—a major challenge in Columbus, Ohio. I finally settled on Carmen's vegetable garden in our community garden and started taking pictures of the flowers she had planted there. From the beginning, I photographed flowers the same way I photographed cats and dogs, with flash and from a low vantage point. I liked the results. I spent the next three years photographing flowers.

I found that overcast, and especially, foggy skies, made for great backdrops, like the neutral gray backdrop in a photographer's studio. It also provided me with a good excuse to spend time in San Francisco doing flower photography.

When I wanted to replicate the black backdrop in a photographer's studio, I photographed flowers at night.

I got a call from Brides magazine in 2013. They had seen a portfolio of my flower pictures on my website, and they liked my approach to flower photography. Would I be interested in being the photographer for their bridal flower arrangement issue? I said I was a photography professor at Ohio State and it was difficult for me to take off. I had classes. I was also thinking that I hadn't done a commercial photography job in years and I was not that eager to do another one. They said we could shoot during the weekend. I said any competent photographer in NYC could copy my style of doing flower pictures. I just shoot up against the sky with a flash. They said we want you to do it. I said I had a lowly 12-megapixel camera. They said that's not a problem. I said it's going to be difficult to shoot in NYC because of the tall buildings will show up in the background. They said we'd rent a building in Brooklyn, and build a platform on the roof. I said what do you pay. I liked what they said. I said count me in. So they built the wooden platform on the roof, provided me with a photo assistant who set up the strobe lights and also put up a tent darkroom on the roof with a monitor where the art director, the photo editor, and the two flower stylists could watch the shoot live. After every shot one of the flower stylists would climb the wood platform and move one of the flowers one inch to the left or to the right. All I did on the shoot was to kneel in front of the flowers, frame the picture, and click the shutter. Afterward, I started thinking I wouldn't mind doing more commercial jobs.

In 2005, Carmen had come to the conclusion that we needed a dog. Lydia, our daughter, was going away to college, and Alex, our son, was already gone. We were about to become empty nesters. Carmen was thinking that at this particular juncture she longed to be showered with love and attention and I was hopeless—a photographer serially obsessed with his current projects. A dog sounded just about right. On a summer morning, we noticed an ad in the paper: Dachshunds For Sale-Six Weeks Old. We drove out from our home in Columbus to a rural farm 40 miles away, thinking it was a nice day for a drive and we would just take a look. When we got there we noticed a long-haired male wandering about by himself. He was alert and friendly and the largest in the litter—the alpha dog. We couldn't resist him. We initially named him Bowie, after David Bowie, because he has a blue eye and a brown eye, but with time his name got shortened to Bob.

Almost overnight, Bob grew up. He turned into a very good dog. Carmen and I became dog nuts. I became Bob's paparazzi. When we planned summer vacations, we only considered beach communities that allowed dogs on the beach without a leash.

Bird, what bird?

Someday, I will catch a squirrel.

Bob has always had a problematic relationship with other dogs. We were noticing that every time we took Bob on his walks, he snarled at every dog we passed. We came to the conclusion that we needed to improve Bob's dog social skills and started taking him to dog parks. Bob's dog park adventure was short-lived. Bob didn't mind the little dogs, but he didn't seem to tolerate the big dogs. Whenever they got close, Bob would start a stare down contest, and I was always afraid he would end up biting the big dog's nose, which happened a couple of times. We gave up trying to socialize Bob.

One happy subset of dog parks is the beach dog park. We discovered a great beach dog park while vacationing in St. Petersburg, Florida, where we witnessed the surreal scene of dozens of dogs on floats.

My cousin Sergio's African Gray parrot, Cucara, is 40 years old. She apparently has forgotten how to fly and her cage door is open all day on the porch of Sergio's Florida Keys home. She's very friendly but if Sergio gets his hand close to her, she will bite him. Sergio clipped her wings once, 39 years ago, and she has not forgotten.

I always wanted to have a parrot, so on a trip to Florida we came back with Coqui, a Quaker parrot who was an accomplished talker. We've never had the heart to cut Coqui's wings. One day I walked outside to grill something and forgot that the parrot was sitting on my shoulder. The moment I stepped out on the deck, Coqui took off. It was her first moment of freedom, and I've never seen a parrot fly so fast. First, straight up, then in circles high above the house, all the while making loud parrot squawks, possibly looking for a mate. Then she landed in a nearby tall tree, made a lot of noise up there, and from there she flew to the next tall tree, and to the next. I followed her on the ground, calling her name. The neighbors all came out, wondering what kind of bird was making such a racket. After one hour of tree hoping, the parrot flew down from one the trees, circled over me, and landed on my shoulder. I grabbed her, took her into the house and put her in her cage again. One year later, the exact same situation happened, but that time, Coqui never returned. I'm hoping she survived.

I think I have taken only two pictures of wild animals, partly because I don't own a telephoto lens and have never wanted to buy one. Almost every picture I've taken has been taken with a wide-angle lens and a flash and I like to get close to what I'm photographing. I was hiking in Costa Rica and this Coati jumped up on the rock, very close to me, almost asking me to take his picture. I did, and the Coati disappeared. On the other instance, I was walking on the Pacific end of Golden Gate Park and a raven inexplicably let me get within a few feet.

In 2016 I starting thinking that maybe I should go to Africa, or the Galapagos, to photograph animals in the wild. Then I learned that it would cost around $6000 to go to Africa on a photo safari and $4000 to go to the Galapagos, and I would end up with pictures that have been done by many others in the past, and by much better nature photographers. Then I thought, it costs $12 to go to the Columbus zoo and I could take as many pictures as I wanted of the animals there. I decided on that course of action. After a few outings at the zoo, I got too depressed watching the animals, and specially, the large apes. They seemed to know they were in some kind of prison. I stopped going to the zoo.

In May 2013, I retired from 25 years of teaching photography at the Ohio State University. Shortly afterward I went to a family wedding in Puerto Rico. I immediately noticed that I had a problem. I was trying to come up with an adequate answer to: what do you do? I didn't particularly want to say: I'm retired. The Puerto Ricans have a better idea. They say: Estoy jubilado. I am jubilated, or I'm in a state of continual jubilation. The American version sounds like you've been shelved. The Puerto Ricans version sounds like: this party is starting!

When I retired from teaching, I had a vague idea that I wanted to travel, but I had no sense of where I wanted to go. As it happened, three nephews got married in rapid succession, all in very interesting places, and I stayed for one week after each wedding to explore and photograph. Jaime got married in Culebra, an island off Puerto Rico, Christopher got married in Alaska, and Carlos go married in Madrid, where I took this picture of my brother, two sisters, and two brother-in-laws, all taking pictures of the bride and groom while the professional wedding photographer takes in the scene and probably worries about the future of his profession.

I went back to Cuba during the summer of 2016 with Carmen and Lydia. Carmen's great aunt, Adamina Maderos, is 92. She lives in Esperanza, a small town near Santa Clara, and we visited her. She laughed easily, and often, and told stories. This is one story she tells: "One day, a friend of my sister comes to our house. She tells me his name is Ignacio. Ignacio looks at me, and tells my sister: you didn't tell me you had a sister! I look at him and I think: he is so good looking! The next day he arrives at our house with his big truck. He comes in and tells me: get in the truck. I say, why? Where are we going? He says, don't worry about where we are going, just get in the truck. I'm thinking: he is so good looking! So I get on the truck and we drive one hour to Cienfuegos. I ask him: what are we going to do in Cienfuegos? He says, don't worry about it. You'll see. So he parks his truck in front of the local judge. He says; we are getting married today. I'm surprised, but he was so good looking! We came back to Esperanza as man and wife."

There is a daily ritual for Havana residents that I particularly like—at the end of the day, they go and sit on the malecón, the seawall that protects Havana from the sea. It's the perfect place for families, friends, and couples to catch the breeze, drink some rum, or go on a date. I sat on the wall for a while, then I decided to photograph everyone sitting within 100 yards of where I was sitting. What I noticed on this trip was how everyone (there was one exception) I photographed sitting on the seawall seemed much happier than when I pursued the same project in 1996.

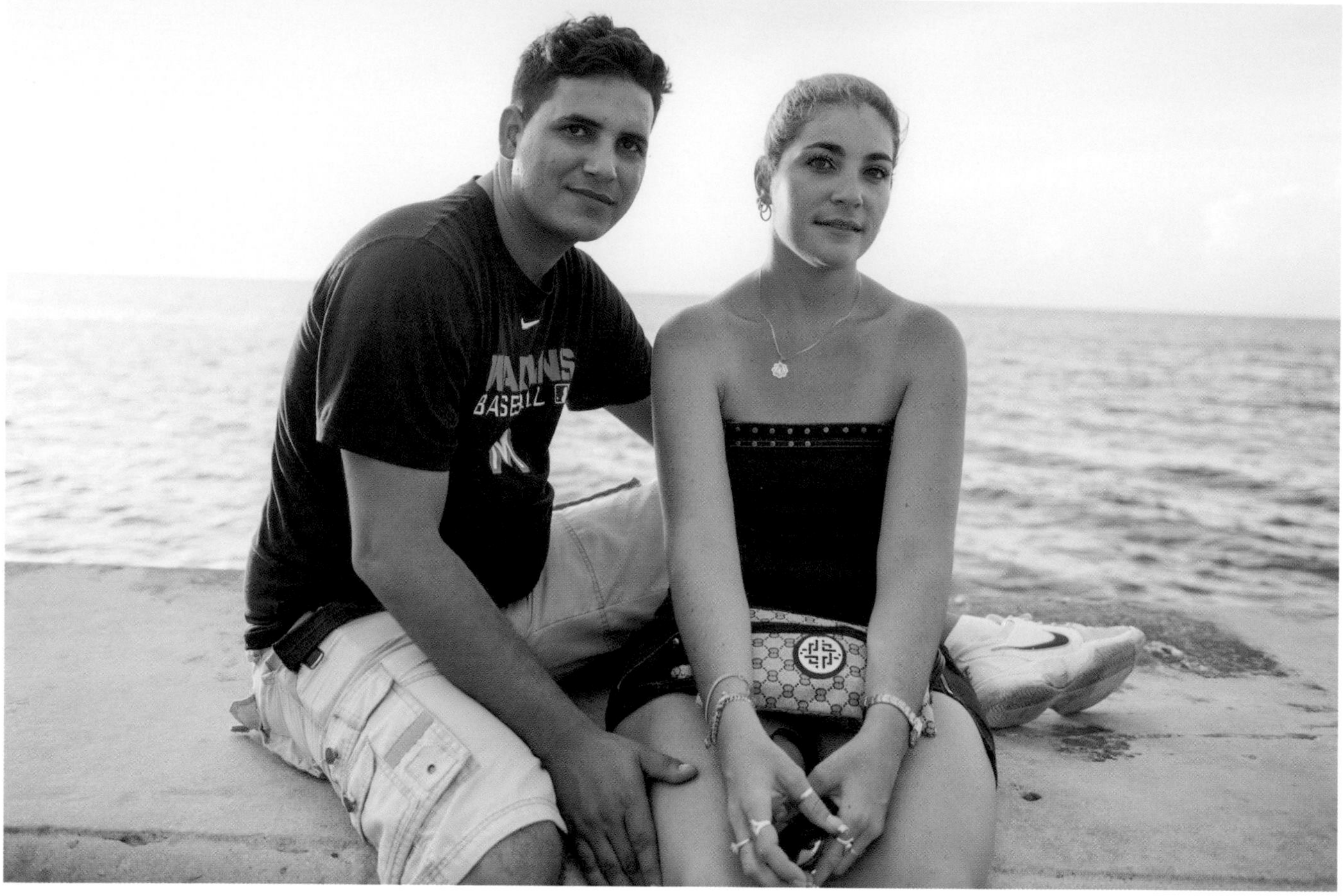
BASEBALL

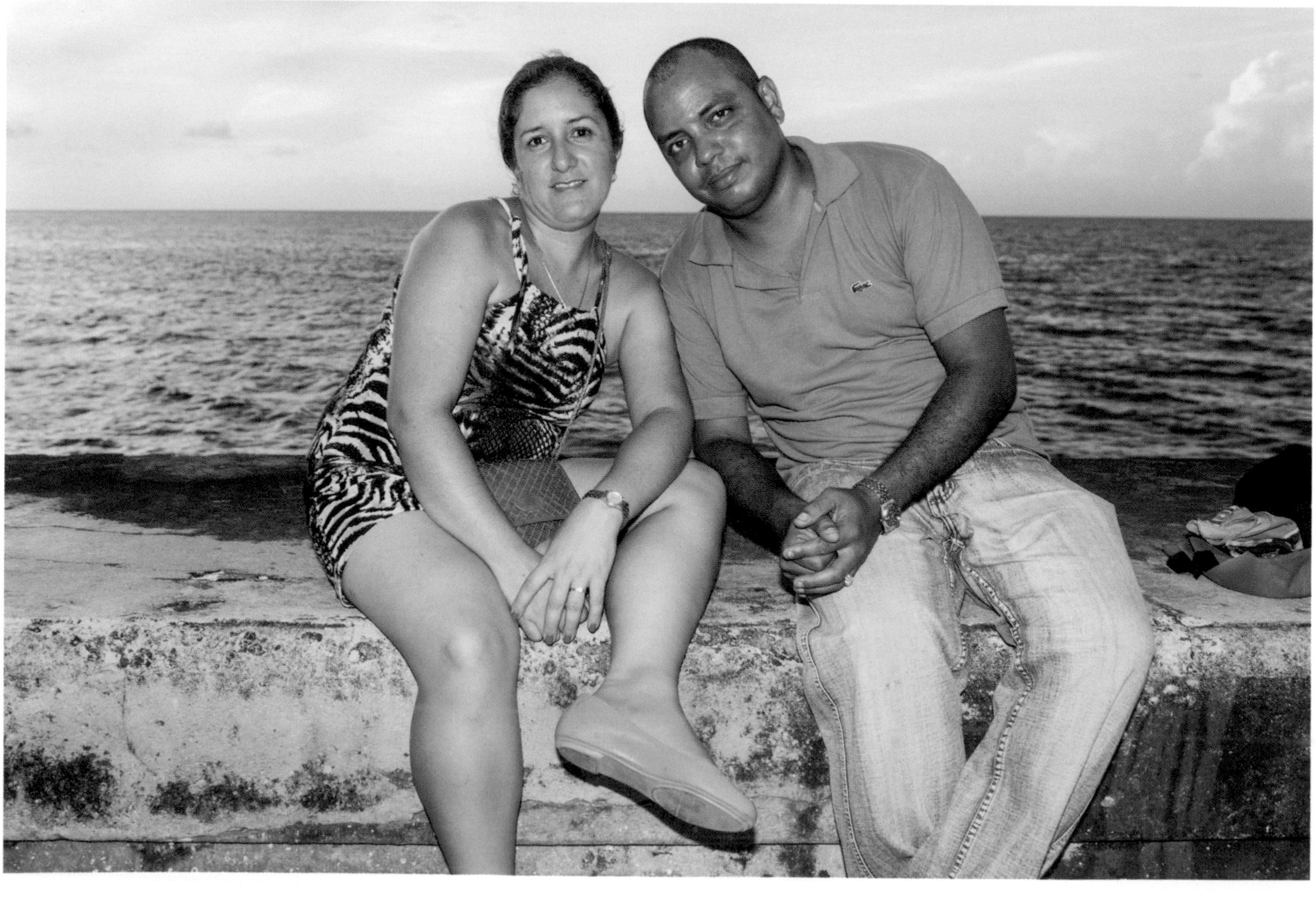

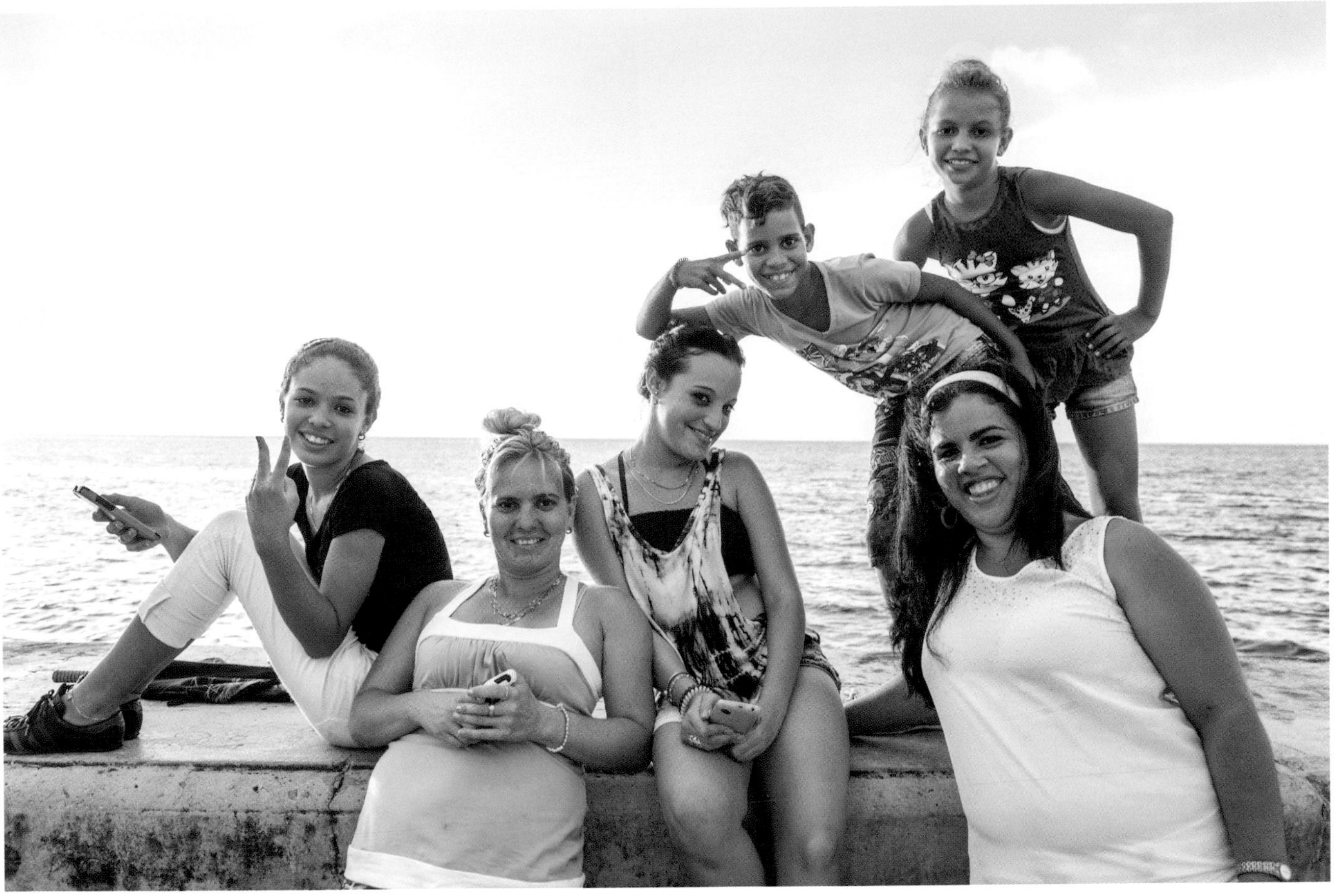

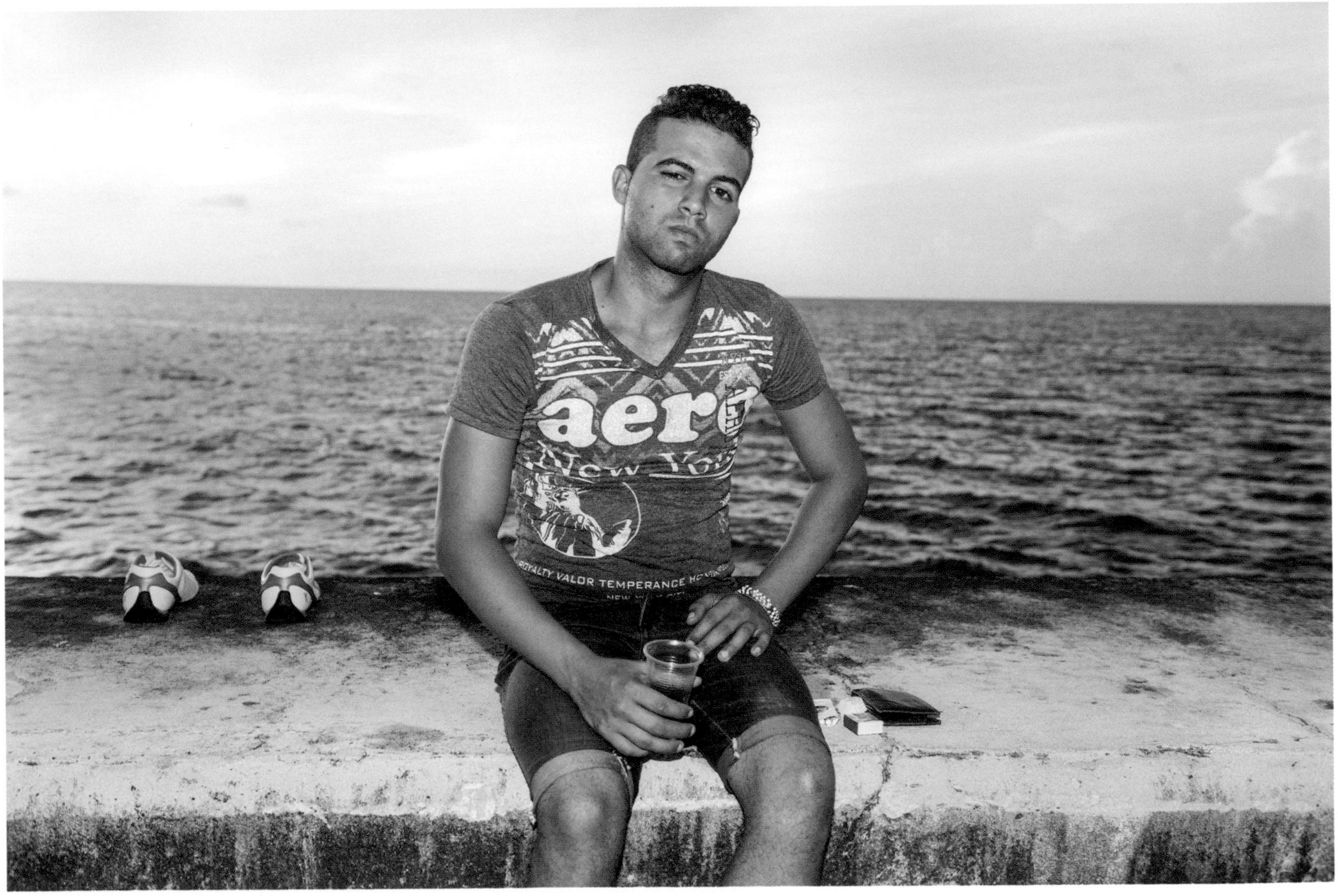
VALOR TEMPERANCE

On my previous trip to Cuba, in 1996, I saw very few cats and the dogs I saw were wild street dogs, all in terrible shape. I was told that there was such a shortage of food during the "special period" that people ate the cats (cat meat tasted like chicken!) and no one could afford to feed their dogs, so they let them loose to fend for themselves. On this trip, the dogs seemed much happier.

Cuban socialism has not been kind to the housing stock throughout Cuba. I walked around my old neighborhood, the Vedado district of Havana, and photographed many of the houses. The rule of thumb about houses in Havana is very simple: if Cuban government officials live (or work) there, the house was a mansion to start with, and it has been renovated and kept up and is currently in perfect condition. If regular Cuban citizens live or work there, it was last repaired in 1960.

My mother's living room, in the house she has lived in for over 50 years. I designed the house when I was a first year architectural student in 1965. On one of the visits to my parents in New Jersey, my father's boss, John Ellis, a friend of the Mendoza brothers from their Yale days, came up to me during a cocktail party.

"Tony," he said, "how would you like to design your parents house?"

"I would love to John," I said, "but I'm pretty sure my father can't afford to build a house."

"No problem," John said. "I own a piece of land nearby and I'll pay for the house."

"Really?" I said, quite amazed. "That's great John! What's my budget?"

"Just design a house that will suit the needs of your family."

The next day I sat down with my parents, so I could come up with a plan for their house. I first interviewed my father. I had a yellow paper pad to write down the list of what he wanted.

"My list is going to be short," he said. "There is only one thing I want. In our bathroom, I want a bidet. Toilet paper is unhygienic." I tried to get more out of him, but that was it.

I thought: OK, my mom will definitely let me know what she wants, especially in the kitchen, the living room, the closets. So I sat down with her, my yellow paper pad at the ready again.

"There is only one thing I want," she said.

"Please don't tell me you want a bidet, because I have that covered."

"On the wall, in our bedroom, by the head of our bed, I want a crucifix that lights up all night."

That was it for her too.

My parents after 54 years of marriage. My father died a few years after this picture was taken, at 80. He lived his health life his way: not exercising (he always drove to get his mail, only 30 yards away at the end of his driveway.) He ate terribly (lunch every day for 30 years at Burgher King!) He smoked, and drank. He only drank scotch, and probably drank scotch every day of his adult life, but to his credit, never before 6pm. When he was 76, he went to his doctor for his yearly physical. He had a million health problems. He had stopped smoking, but now his doctor told him something he didn't want to hear: "Miguel, you have to stop drinking." My father replied that he preferred to be dead than to give up his scotch. His doctor then said: "OK. But can you promise me to just have one drink a day?" My father thought about it, and after a long pause, agreed. He left the doctor's office and drove to Woolworth, where he remembered having seen some very large plastic glasses. He kept his promise to his doctor. He drank only one (gigantic) scotch a day until the day he died.

I wish I had stories to tell about the people in this painting of my 19th century Mendoza family, but those stories have been lost because no one wrote them down. I'm named after the gentleman on the far right, my great, great grandfather, Antonio Gonzales de Mendoza. That Antonio might have been the last very illustrious member of my family. He headed the top law firm of his time, taught law at the University of Havana, was the first Cuban landowner to liberate his slaves, was elected mayor of Havana, and in 1899, shortly after Cuba gained its independence, he was named the first Chief Justice of the Cuban Supreme Court. He had twelve children, portrayed in this 1886 painting, and seven eventually married and started their own families, but in those days when the children married, they didn't move out; the family complex in Amargura Street in Old Havana just got bigger. At the peak, there were 53 grandchildren living in the Mendoza complex, which occupied close to an entire city block. My father grew up there in the Twenties, with thirty first cousins. They ate at what was referred to as the "little table," which was still large enough to serve the 30 first cousins and their 15 nannies. After school, my father recalled, there were enough first cousins to field two baseball teams. The children moved to the "big table" when they were around 15, and had reached an acceptable level of table manners and conversation. My father told a story about being demoted back to the little table after his first day at the big table, after an incident that involved his attempt to get to the meat of a stone crab's claw.

Every five years the descendants of Antonio Gonzales de Mendoza (1828-1906) and Chea Pedroso (1835-1895) have a family reunion in Miami. The last four reunions have taken place at the Biltmore Hotel in Coral Gables. There are two days of socializing and games, culminating in a dinner and dance, and of course, a family picture, which perfectly explains the world's overpopulation. Each of Don Antonio's seven married children started a branch, and the descendants of the seven branches each wear a different color polo shirt. The attendance lately to these reunions have numbered around 800, with family members showing up from all over the US, South America, and a few from Europe. I started going to these reunions during the Seventies, when I was single. I could go up to any attractive girl I didn't know and break the ice by saying: Hi Cousin! On the 2012 reunion there were a large number of young single people, and they were partying all over in the Biltmore Hotel after the official functions ended. The young crowd was texting family members asking the same question: how far removed does one have to be to be a kissing cousin? The consensus answer was that 2nd cousins were fair game—anyone not wearing the color of your polo shirt.

My mom was 97 when she fell down as she was entering Sunday Mass and broke
her left femur bone. She had surgery the next day. I was the only family member
there, so the surgeon asked me, just before the operation: had she had any problem
with anesthesia in the past? It was hard for me, or for my mother, to answer that
question. Her last operation with anesthesia was an appendicitis operation when she
was eight, 89 years ago. He said, OK, that was a long time ago, but we have to do it,
and the operation went well. The day after, when I took this picture, she seems to be
in good spirits, and she made a remarkable recovery. She had surgery on a Monday,
started walking a few paces with a walker on Tuesday, left the hospital on Thursday,
and moved to an intensive rehabilitation center for a week before moving back to
her home. I stayed in her house the first week with Lily, her 90-year-old in dog-years
poodle, who normally sleeps in the same bed with my mother. Every night that week I
would wake up in the middle of the night to the loud howlings of Lily, crying frantically
because my mother was not in her bed.

My mother six months after her operation, looking very hip at 98, enjoying a
Corona at a rooftop bar in the Jersey Shore.

When Lydia lived at home, Carmen and Lydia loved shopping together. One day at Macy's, Lydia was trying on a dress for her high school's Father-Daughter dance. Carmen loved the dress. She said: you have to get it! Lydia agreed because she thought it made her look Latin. She ran around the dressing room singing, "I feel pretty" from West Side Story. She also thought it was too expensive and refused to let Carmen buy it. Carmen insisted. Finally, Carmen convinced Lydia when she said: I have a coupon at home, it will be much cheaper, we'll put it on hold, and we'll come back tomorrow. They went back to Macy's the next day. When they asked for the dress, the sales-woman brought it out and said: there was a woman in the dressing room who saw Lydia wearing the dress, overheard your conversation, and was moved by it. She bought the dress for her and wants to remain anonymous. Almost instantly, Carmen and Lydia started crying.

Our two children, Alex and Lydia, like most young people today, have plenty of professional and romantic problems. Every time they are worried about a current disappointment in those areas, I'm always tempted to tell them: you are focusing on a minor detail, focus on the big picture: you are young, you are smart, you are educated, you are attractive, and you have your life ahead of you.

Picture by Carmen Mendoza 2017

Tony Mendoza was born in Havana, Cuba in 1941. He left for Miami with his family in the summer of 1960, when it became clear that Fidel's revolution intended to turn Cuba into a socialist state. He bought his first camera, a Kodak Brownie, at eleven and continued to take pictures through grammar school, high school, Yale University (Bachelor of Engineering, 1963) and the Harvard Graduate School of Design (Master of Architecture, 1968.) In 1973, to the dismay of his creditors and relatives, he turned full time to the pursuit of photography as art. Since then, his work has been exhibited and published widely. He has received three National Endowment for the Arts Photography Fellowships, a Guggenheim Photography Fellowship, and five Ohio Arts Council Fellowships in photography, creative writing, and video. His photographs are included in the collections of many museums, including the Museum of Modern Art, New York, the San Francisco Museum of Modern Art, The Metropolitan Museum of Art, New York, the LA County Museum of Art, the Museum of Fine Arts, Boston, the Fogg Musuem, Harvard University, and the Columbus Museum of Art.. He tsught photography at the Ohio State University for 25 years and now hopes to resume his career as a full time artist.

Other Books by Tony Mendoza

A Cuban Summer
Capra Press 2013
A coming-of-age novel set in Cuba in 1954

Flowers
Nazraeli Press 2007
A book of flower pictures taken from a low vantage point

Ernie: A Photographer's Memoir
Chronicle Books 2001
A book of pictures and stories about Ernie, a cat

Cuba: Going Back
University of Texas Press 1999
A book about my first trip back to Cuba after 36 years of exile.

Dog Postcards
Capra Press 1995
A book of dog postcards

Ernie's Postcard Book
Capra Press 1889
A book of Ernie postcards

Stories
Atlantic Monthly Press 1987
A book of pictures with attached short stories

Ernie: A Photographer's Memoir
Capra Press 1985
The original Ernie book

Thank You!

To all of you who contributed to the successful Kickstarter campaign which made this book possible.

Bob Doyle • Sergio Andres Mendoza • Carlos Carillo • Mike Hazard • Lydia Ana Mendoza • Mario G Mendoza • Judy Gelles • Annie Marie Musselman • Anne Tucker • Aline Smithson • Casey Vincent • Constance Brinkley • Martin Osborn • Stephen McAteer • Noelle McCleaf • Annie Mejer • Celso Gonzales-Falla • Cheri Harrison • Jean Jackson • Marianne York • Sergio Mendoza • Jim Graves • Stacy Baumgarn.• Jaclyn Silverman • Henry Horenstein • M. Salome Galib • Susan T. Landry• Sylvia Gardner • Joan Morgenstern • Rebecca Ibel • Elsie Sanchez • Katherine Martin Widmer • Andres Duany • Pam Edwards • Peter Tarasewich • Barbara Buell • Migiwa Orimo• Felicia Murray • Sarah Allen • Ruthie Newcomer • Lisa Dush • Lysa Hoffman • Skeet McCauley • Terry Barrett • Jeremy Jorgenson • Sharon Francis • Henry Little • Cristi Mendoza Edmunds • John Broughton • Ashley Corkum • Barb Vogel • Luke Snailham • Sharon Fox • Amy Firestone • Will Loxton • Domingo de Montejo • Paul Balser • Constantine Cacos • Jennifer Dush • Michael Reese • Gillie Campbell • Travis Hoewischer • Julie Snow • Lawrence Lipkin • Christopher Rauschenberg • Simon Robinson • Erica Berger • Ann Kendellen • Ines Maruri • Dennis Fallon • Phillipe Gross • Sheri Blaney • Mosquera Orthodontics • Andrew Rosenthal • Trinity Shi • • Jerry Friedman • Tommy N. Armansyah • Peggy Nolan